TO SAM WISEMAN,
ALL THE BEST.

Roger Hart

11-2-06

POSTCARDS FROM DETROIT

POSTCARDS FROM DETROIT

REMEMBERING FORMULA I IN THE MOTOR CITY

BY ROGER HART

DESIGN BY TOM MORGAN

DAVID BULL PUBLISHING

To my wife Lisa who never seemed to mind giving up many of her summer weekends as her husband was off taking pictures of race cars.

Library of Congress Control Number: 2006928483

ISBN: 1 893618 72 2

David Bull Publishing, logo, and colophon are trademarks of David Bull Publishing, Inc.

Book and cover design: Tom Morgan, Blue Design, Portland, Maine

Printed in Hong Kong

10 9 8 7 6 5 4 3 2 1

David Bull Publishing
4250 East Camelback Road
Suite K150
Phoenix, AZ 85018

602-852-9500
602-852-9503 (fax)

www.bullpublishing.com

PAGE 2: With fresh Goodyears mounted, Ayrton Senna waits for qualifying with his John Player Special Team Lotus crew. The 1986 event began a three-race string of Motown wins for the Brazilian. I love this photo for the relaxed look Senna has while sitting in the Lotus, the umbrella shading him from the sun, and the crew member sitting on the tire. Just another Saturday afternoon.

RIGHT: In 1987, Lotus received Honda power, and it helped propel Ayrton Senna to the winner's circle in Detroit. From my perch in the tower at the end of the main straight, I could make pan shots with a long lens as cars raced through the first corner. A corner worker I met years after this race commented that he watched Senna hit the exact same spot in the first turn for each of the race's 63 laps.

PAGE 6: The gleaming Renaissance Center as a backdrop instantly identifies the location of this photo, although the driver, Oscar Larrauri, remains unknown to all but the most ardent F1 fans. Larrauri, driving for the Euro Brun-Ford team, failed to qualify for most of the races in 1988, but he did make it into the Detroit field, retiring with gearbox failure after 26 laps.

CONTENTS

RACING IN THE STREETS

Detroit and Monaco are worlds apart, but for seven consecutive years from 1982 through 1988, both played host to Formula 1 races run on a course through city streets. You would be hard-pressed to find similarities other than both being located near water, but even then, comparison between the two is a stretch. Detroit, perhaps the poster child for American Midwestern Rust Belt cities, is located along the Detroit River, which separates it from Canada, while the principality of Monaco, a playground for the rich and famous that is presided over by a royal family, looks out on the Mediterranean Sea. Worlds apart indeed.

In 1982, the Formula 1 race in Detroit counted just as much toward the world championship as did Monaco, the sport's crown jewel. Detroit had won a spot on the F1 calendar without having first hosted a non-points-counting race, an unusual allowance for the day. In 1982, Detroit and the State of Michigan were hurting from an economic recession, and the auto industry had been hit hard by rising fuel prices and increased competition from imported cars. Unemployment rates in the city and the state were high. In the midst of the economic doom and gloom that surrounded them, city fathers thought having colorful race cars driven by drivers whose names few within the city would recognize was a signal the city was coming back.

The Detroit race had several fathers who were responsible for making it happen. Collectively, the group was known as Detroit Renaissance, and it was made up of community leaders who came together to try and turn the city around following the race riots of the 1960s. Detroit Renaissance, made

OPPOSITE: Formula 1 racing in Detroit got under way on June 6, 1982, with pole sitter Alain Prost in a Renault, right, leading the way toward the first turn trying to hold off a charging Keke Rosberg. This was the "money shot" I was hired to deliver. Eventual race winner John Watson, who started the race from the 17th position, cannot be seen in this photo of the start.

up of CEOs of some of Detroit's largest corporations, was led by industrialist Henry Ford II, philanthropist Max Fisher, and banker Robert Surdam. These three, along with Detroit Renaissance president Robert McCabe, also known as Champagne Bob, were largely responsible for bringing Formula One racing to Motor City.

Detroit, home to the Big Three vehicle manufacturers at the time—GM, Ford, and Chrysler—was not unfamiliar with racing. Woodward Avenue, which stretches from the heart of downtown all the way out to the suburbs, was a place for street drag racers to test their machinery. Urban legend is rampant with stories about car company engineers trying out their latest go-faster products in test cars they ran up and down Woodward. Even Henry Ford made a name for himself by winning a race in nearby Grosse Pointe that helped solidify funding for his fledgling company—allowing him to revolutionize the industry.

So hosting a major race in the city synonymous the world over with the auto industry would seem to be a good idea.

In fact, it was a good idea, although the 2.5-mile, 20-turn circuit through bumpy Detroit streets was probably not the best venue in which to showcase the greatest racing cars and racing drivers in the world. The logistical problems associated with running a street race through a major city—the closing of sections of main streets for days while barriers were erected and bleachers constructed—upset the daily lives of thousands of people. Newspaper and television accounts that first year showed businesspeople climbing over concrete barriers and through holes in steel fences to get to work. And parking, well, that was another problem. For thousands of Detroiters to endure all of that hassle only to be greeted by these foreigners coming to town and complaining about the circuit and the city was a turnoff. But despite the difficulties and the culture clash, news reports estimated the race day crowd at around 75,000 fans, so all was not lost.

One of the goals city leaders had was to showcase Detroit as an international city capable of hosting a world-class event, and to that extent, despite a few hiccups along the way, the race was a success. Magnificent Formula 1 cars running around the gleaming towers of Detroit's Renaissance Center, constructed in 1977 as a symbol of the city's rebirth, looked great on worldwide television. No matter that the buildings themselves were like mazes with visitors telling stories of getting lost inside the big towers.

At the time of the race, Detroit was enjoying its role of playing host to a string of national

John Watson gets ready for a wet practice run prior to the 1982 race. "In practice the car wasn't working very good—in fact it was bloody awful," Watson said about his McLaren. "I didn't expect to be able to overtake anyone in the race. But I found I could brake a little later and still keep grip." The Detroit victory was one of the five he racked up in 154 Grands Prix.

events. The Republican National Convention took place downtown in 1980; delegates nominated Ronald Reagan for the presidency. Two years later, the National Football League's Super Bowl was staged in suburban Pontiac. Then on June 4, 1982, Formula 1 came to Detroit. Advertising slogans of the day called Detroit SuperCity USA.

My entrance ticket to take the photographs in this book can be traced back nearly a year before that first Detroit Grand Prix. In July 1981, I was part of the Associated Press photo crew covering the Michigan 500 CART race at Michigan International Speedway (MIS), located about 75 miles west of downtown Detroit. At the time, I was just one year out of Central Michigan University and working as a photographer at a weekly newspaper in Caro, Michigan. As a fan, I had always been interested in racing, having grown up just 30 minutes south of MIS. I attended a few races at the speedway, and a colleague suggested I join him as part of the AP crew shooting the race. I made the long drive from Caro to MIS for that first race, and as part of the 10-plus-person team, I drew the assignment of standing in one of the turns, waiting for a wreck. It wasn't glamorous, but I was excited to be part of the crew covering big-time auto racing.

The race was rained out and rescheduled for a week later. I came back the next week, although several other stringers, as the freelance shooters are known, could not make it, and I was given the job of climbing to the top of the press box to cover the first and fourth turns and pit lane with an 800 mm telephoto lens. I had never worked with a lens longer than 300 mm before that day, so I was a little bit nervous about this assignment. I knew it was a big responsibility, and with this my first racing job, I didn't want to blow it.

So I ventured to the top of the grandstand press box with my cameras and the AP's 800 mm lens, a borrowed motor-driven Nikon, and a tripod. I also had a two-way radio to communicate with the photo editor who was working out of a darkroom set up in a trailer in the infield. Early in the race, a pit fire broke out when Herm Johnson brought his car in for a refueling stop. I motor-drived a roll of film as smoke billowed from his car, and the photo I made of a safety worker dousing Johnson with a bucket of water moved out on the AP wire. A majority of newspapers around the country published it the next day, and I awoke two

days before my 23rd birthday to see the photo on the front page of the *Detroit Free Press* and even bigger on the front page of the sports section of the *Detroit News*. I had earned my first stripe as a racing photographer.

With that photo in my portfolio, I was able to join the 20 or so people making up the AP crew covering the first Detroit Renaissance Grand Prix. Because of my ability to capture the pit fire photo at MIS, I became known as a "racing photographer," a moniker I was proud to have. Because of that, I was given the race day assignment of shooting from a tower in the first turn, looking down the front straightaway alongside the Detroit River.

The start of a Formula 1 race is arguably the most exciting and dangerous time of the race. I knew the pressure was on me to make sure I had the photo if something were to happen. But because that position would be staffed only on race day, I talked my way into getting to shoot from the pits for the two qualifying days before the race. I convinced the photo editor, who would later become a good friend, that I understood racing and should get the assignment.

No question about it, both of these assignments, working the pits during qualifying and shooting from the tower on race day, were plum. Most of the AP photographers were covering corners, waiting for "incidents" of cars contacting the wall. For all seven F1 races in Detroit, this was my routine: Friday and Saturday, I worked the pits during practice and qualifying, occasionally getting a chance to walk around some of the circuit, then the stint in the turn one tower for the race. During practice and qualifying, unless there was a crash in a corner, the majority of the photos sent out on the AP wire came from the pits. Candid shots of drivers and their cars were what photo editors wanted. But in seven years of covering this race, shooting more than 100 rolls of film, only about 30 or so of my photos were ever published. Until now.

So, you will not see any photos of race winners spraying champagne or hoisting a trophy or being kissed by a beauty queen. I never had a chance to shoot victory circle. The closest thing I have to a celebration shot is a driver raising a hand acknowledging the checkered flag. And it was not until Formula 1 abandoned Detroit and the race was run with cars and drivers from CART that I had a chance to shoot what became a signature shot from the race: a car making a turn in front of the *Spirit of Detroit* sculpture.

What is contained in this book are photos of a bygone era, one that is gone not only from Detroit but from Formula 1 racing. One of the reasons among many that F1 left Detroit was that race organizers would not commit to building permanent garages to house the teams, a requirement Formula 1 management made of all its tracks. Like Monaco, also a temporary circuit, the pits were wide open, and teams had to ferry the race cars from the paddock area, which was in a parking garage beneath the Renaissance Center, to pit lane. At F1 racetracks today, pit lane is lined with garages that house the team's race operations, atop of which are suites that house the circuit's Paddock Club, where tickets cost several thousand dollars each.

Another reason given at the time was that construction in downtown Detroit made laying out the racetrack impossible. That's true today, but it took more than a decade after Formula 1 left Detroit before that construction took place, and swallowed up parts of the track.

When Formula 1 arrived in Detroit, it was a sport undergoing tremendous change. Formula 1's Turbo Era was in its infancy, when 1.5-liter turbocharged cars were churning out upwards of 750hp (some would argue the turbo cars were making upwards of 1000hp!) in qualifying trim versus the 510hp made by the venerable 3.0-liter Cosworth V8. Turbo-powered cars were the class of the field, but Detroit did hold a few surprises, and as they say, that is why the race is run.

After the final F1 event in 1988, I photographed the CART races in the streets of Detroit, then later on Belle Isle, an island in the middle of the Detroit River where the event moved, but the magic was gone. It was no longer the United States Grand Prix but just another stop on the CART calendar. Yes, the names of the drivers were more familiar, with the likes of Foyt and Andretti and Unser. And you could argue, the racing, the actual competition, was better with CART than it ever was with Formula 1. But true CART fans could venture west to MIS to see an even better show where the CART cars would spin for hours around the 2-mile track at speeds of more than 200 mph.

When F1 left downtown Detroit, so did the spark that is so hard to define yet so instantly recognizable when you feel it. The electricity that is in the air when 20 colorful, powerful race cars roll up to a starting grid ready for the race to begin is pure magic, and one of the drawing cards of the sport. Formula 1 fans know that spark. These photos of Formula 1's 21 magical days in Detroit are for you.

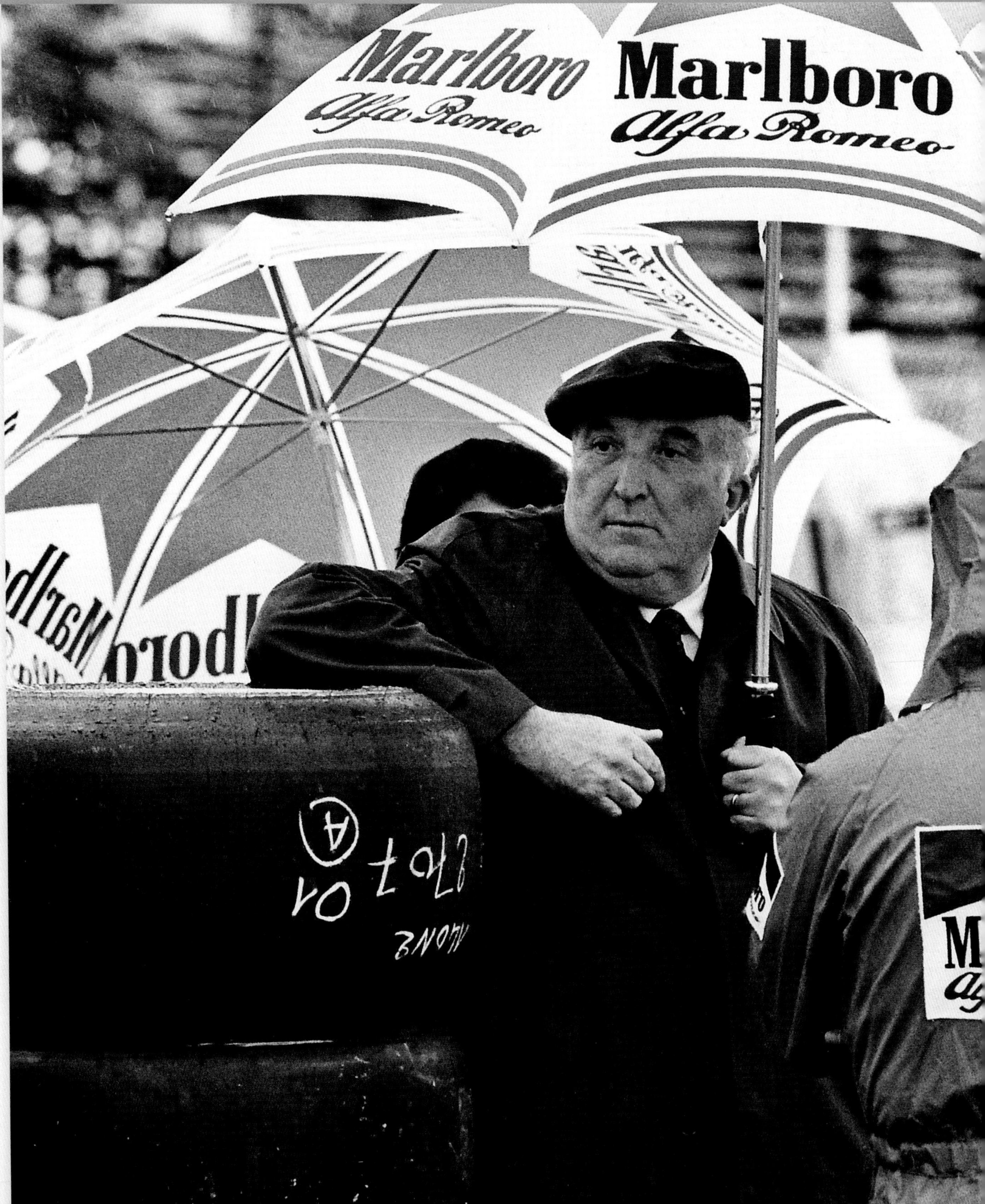
Marlboro
Alfa Romeo
Marlboro
Alfa Romeo

CHAPTER I

THE ATMOSPHERE

Rain during a motor race is rarely a good thing, but during practice for the first Detroit Grand Prix, it resulted in one of my favorite photos. Alfa Romeo's team leader Carlo Chiti took refuge beneath an umbrella prior to a practice session that would be run in the rain. When I approached him to ask him for his name—standard operating procedure for an AP photographer—he scoffed and said, "Don't you know who I am? And you are a motoring journalist?" He eventually gave me his name.

OPPOSITE: A lot of familiar faces have been associated with Formula 1 through the years, but few people have tirelessly supported the sport like three-time world champion Jackie Stewart. During the first Detroit Grand Prix, he was everywhere talking about the sport—even though he had retired from the cockpit some time before. Stewart was said to have been responsible for convincing drivers not to walk out after the track did not initially meet all the safety criteria required.

ABOVE LEFT: Newspapers and magazines were not quite as celebrity hungry as they are today, but even in 1982 a supermodel and her race driver/heir-to-a-fortune boyfriend were newsworthy. Christie Brinkley, with a beautiful Leica camera around her neck, was in Detroit to watch then boyfriend Olivier Chandon participate in one of the support races during the weekend. Less than a year later, Chandon, heir to the Moet-Chandon champagne fortune, would die while testing a Formula Atlantic car at Moroso Park in Florida.

ABOVE RIGHT: Getting around the downtown Detroit racetrack could be a bit of a hassle on race day, as these fans learned filing out of the track.

OPPOSITE: If there is one thing I've learned in more than 20 years hanging around racetracks it is that there is a lot of downtime. Crew members are under extreme pressure to get the cars prepared, and when it's done, there's not much else to do but take a load off and relax. Work time would come soon enough.

ABOVE: Nigel Mansell became known among the local Detroit media as a good quote and in his best Queen's English was not afraid to say what was on his mind. His battles with Ayrton Senna for pole position during the last couple of years of the event were worth the price of admission. Though he never finished better than fifth (he did it twice: 1986 and 1987), Mansell always talked like a champion. Four years after the last Detroit race, Mansell would claim his one and only world championship.

FOLLOWING PAGES: This photo received a fair bit of play in newspapers around the country because it's just not something you see every day. Mechanics are usually scrambling to get cars prepared to race, not using them as back supports for a rest. What I especially like about the photo are the tick-tack-toe marks on the asphalt and the stocking feet of the two mechanics.

OPPOSITE: Paul Newman was not only an accomplished actor but a pretty good shoe as well. He drove in the Sports Car Club of America's Trans-Am race during the Grand Prix weekend. Because the Trans-Am practices followed the F1 track time, few press photographers stuck around to see the race or get this photo. It's another one of my favorites.

ABOVE: Paul Newman is famously shy about dealing with the media, and for the most part during his appearances in Detroit, he would get in his car in the safety of the paddock and have the car pushed to pit lane to avoid the media crush. Having a Hollywood face in town helped contribute to the glamour factor that was the Detroit Grand Prix.

By 1988, the pit lane in Detroit featured small covered work areas that offered a little bit of protection for the team's equipment—a far cry from the full garages found at all the circuits today. But the staging area in pit lane was beginning to change, meaning less access to the media and fans. Here, the McLarens of Alain Prost, right, and Ayrton Senna wait for qualification to begin. At the far left is McLaren team boss Ron Dennis.

Mario Andretti seemed to be an interested spectator at nearly all the Detroit Grands Prix. Here he talks with fellow Italian Teo Fabi, who in 1984 was attempting to race in both F1 and CART, with his brother Corrado filling in for him when race dates overlapped. Maybe talking to the 1978 world champion did some good, as Fabi, driving for Brabham, finished on the podium in third place in 1984, his best finish ever in F1.

OPPOSITE: Danny Sullivan made a triumphant return to Detroit in 1985 as the winner of the Indianapolis 500. Here he's showing off the ring presented to the winner of that race to some Lotus mechanics. Sullivan drove in Detroit during his one year in Formula 1 in 1983; he retired from the race with electrical problems.

ABOVE LEFT: One usually associates race ambassador Linda Vaughn with either stock car or drag racing, but she was in Detroit in 1983. Here she chats with CART driver Bobby Rahal. Both were working the pits prior to qualifying.

ABOVE RIGHT: Nigel Mansell's Williams-Honda crew goes over the car prior to qualifying for the 1987 race. The crew had pushed the car out of its pit stall and down pit lane to get in line to wait for the track to go green. The Renaissance Center in the background is a massive four-tower office complex that surrounds a 73-story hotel tower in the middle.

TOP RIGHT: The Detroit Grand Prix was a chance for old friends to get together again. Here, 1982 world champion Keke Rosberg talks with CART driver Howdy Holmes, right, and Doug Shierson, owner of the Domino's Pizza CART team for which Holmes drove. Shierson, Holmes, and Rosberg had known each other for some time, having competed in Formula Atlantic races. Years later, Shierson, from Adrian, Michigan, would go to victory lane at the Indianapolis Motor Speedway with driver Arie Luyendyk. Shierson came to be a good friend and mentor to me and was one of the first people I spoke with after being offered the managing editor job at *AutoWeek*.

RIGHT: In the later years of the Detroit Grand Prix, Motown became known as Little Brazil during the race weekend, as thousands of Brazilians would flock to the city to cheer on their hero, Ayrton Senna. They had a lot to cheer about as Senna won the race three times, spurred on by those waving Brazilian and Senna flags and numerous fans.

Ayrton Senna takes his Lotus-Renault down pit lane in preparation for a practice run. For 51 weeks of the year, pit lane was actually a parking lot behind the towering Renaissance Center. Today the area is part of a massive river walk program that was started by the City of Detroit and General Motors, whose world headquarters now occupies much of the RenCen.

CHAPTER 2

THE CONTENDERS

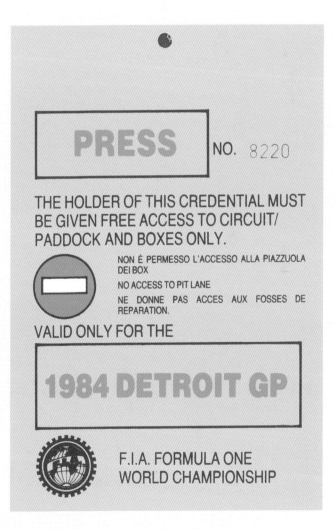

PRESS NO. 8220

THE HOLDER OF THIS CREDENTIAL MUST BE GIVEN FREE ACCESS TO CIRCUIT/ PADDOCK AND BOXES ONLY.

NON È PERMESSO L'ACCESSO ALLA PIAZZUOLA DEI BOX
NO ACCESS TO PIT LANE
NE DONNE PAS ACCES AUX FOSSES DE REPARATION.

VALID ONLY FOR THE

1984 DETROIT GP

F.I.A. FORMULA ONE WORLD CHAMPIONSHIP

Don't think Formula 1 drivers are pampered? Here, one crew member holds an umbrella while another dries off the shoes of Alain Prost before he straps in for a qualifying run. Wet shoes on the pedals would not be a good thing. Although trying to keep camera equipment dry was a challenge during these rain showers, I always enjoyed shooting this race during the few times it rained. Rain had a way of clearing out pit lane, leaving only those people who really had to be there—all the hangers-on headed for cover.

OPPOSITE: Of the thousands of photos I shot during the Formula 1 races in Detroit, this is my absolute favorite—funny it has so little to do with racing. Jacques Laffite reacts in laughter after telling a joke to Keke Rosberg. I wasn't close enough to hear what was said and I was able to make only one frame before the mood changed, but this, to me, represents what was right about Formula 1 in the 1980s: it was a big business and lives were on the line each and every race, but there was still fun in it.

ABOVE: Twenty-seven-year-old Alain Prost prepares to head out for a wet practice session for the inaugural Detroit Grand Prix. Prost sat on pole for that first race and had the race in hand before a mechanical problem dropped him to 12th place.

BELOW: Rene Arnoux had just climbed from the cockpit of his Ferrari after winning the pole for the 1983 race when Formula 1 majordomo Bernie Ecclestone—wearing the uniform of his Brabham team—swept him up to lead him to the postqualifying press conference. Arnoux looks a bit bewildered, but Ecclestone's guiding hand is very much evident.

ABOVE LEFT: Italian Elio de Angelis, beneath the protection of an umbrella, prepares to head out in his Lotus for practice in the wet prior to the 1983 race. Known as a gentleman racer, de Angelis finished second in the 1984 race.

ABOVE RIGHT: The Team Lotus brain trust, including Lotus team boss Peter Warr (bending down), communicates prior to Elio de Angelis's taking to the track in 1984. One of the things that differed between Formula 1 and open-wheel racing in the United States was how the team members would have to plug their headsets into the driver's helmet to create an intercom, rather than relying on two-way radio communications. Usually the team manager would plug his headset into the driver's helmet and then start a daisy chain with other team members linking up.

OPPOSITE: A race car cockpit would seem to be an odd place to catch a bit of shut-eye, but Eddie Cheever had no problem relaxing in his Alfa Romeo prior to practice for the 1984 race.

ABOVE LEFT: Race car drivers and pretty women go hand in hand. One of two American-born drivers to race F1 in Detroit, American Eddie Cheever, who raced in all seven Detroit Grands Prix, is here with his wife, Rita. His second-place finish in 1982 driving a Ligier-Matra was his best-ever finish in F1. Even today, Cheever says he should have won the race.

ABOVE RIGHT: Martin Brundle, left, and Eddie Cheever talk before qualifying for the 1987 race. Brundle was driving for Zakspeed, and Cheever had moved on to the Arrows-Megatron team, the fifth team he drove for in the seven years of the Detroit race. The 1987 event was not kind to Brundle, who retired from the race with mechanical problems. Cheever went on to finish sixth.

: Rene Arnoux appears to have a headache, but he was actually signaling his Ligier team that he was having trouble hearing them through the two-way communication system. Arnoux was waiting for adjustments to be made prior to qualifying for the 1986 race.

LEFT: Seeing drivers sitting in their cars without their helmets is always a bit jarring—something is not quite right. During this era of Formula 1, it was common for drivers to climb into the car, get strapped in, and then wait to don their helmets just prior to heading out on the track. Here, Gerhard Berger waits in his Ferrari as the team tends to the car. He finished fourth in 1987, the last car on the lead lap.

ABOVE: Stefan Johansson's McLaren MP4 gets some last-minute service work before practice for the 1987 race. Three crew members are holding up the bodywork as mechanics tend to the car's engine. Despite what appears to be dry weather, the McLaren is shod with rain tires. Crews would routinely install rain tires on the car for the pushout from the paddock to pit lane, where slicks would then be put on the car.

OPPOSITE: In 1987, Stefan Johansson was teamed with the 1985 and '86 world champion Alain Prost at McLaren, and there was no doubt he was playing second fiddle on the team. Johansson finished second in the Detroit race the previous year in a Ferrari but could do no better than seventh place in 1987, three laps behind Ayrton Senna's Lotus-Honda.

OPPOSITE: Patrick Tambay has a drink of water while waiting for qualifying for the 1984 race. Notice the little sticker to the right of his head—it's from the Sports Car Club of America. SCCA members, who normally were working regional events, came to Detroit in droves and worked as marshals and inspectors. The sticker signifies that the Renault had successfully passed inspection.

LEFT: The best year of competition in the Detroit Grand Prix was probably 1988, with McLaren teammates Alain Prost and Ayrton Senna waging a battle to the end. Senna won with Prost second, 38 seconds behind. One of the big rumors that year was that despite having equally prepared cars, Prost and Senna were getting slightly different fuel blends, with an advantage going to Senna. Here, Prost's McLaren gets topped off. I remember the mixture smelled more like perfume than gasoline. Note McLaren designer Gordon Murray in the left background wearing the headset.

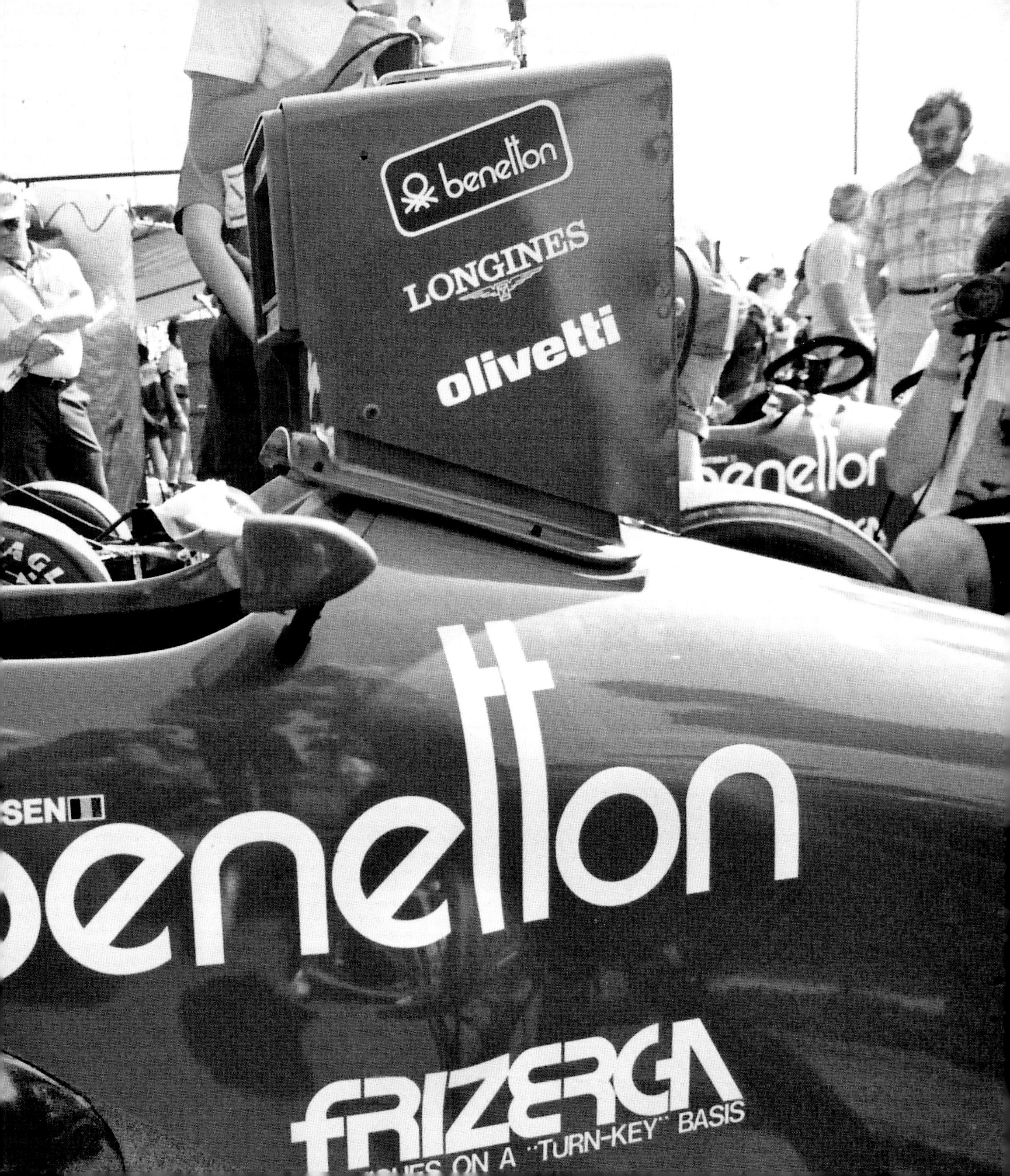
benetton
LONGINES
olivetti
FRIZERGA
"TURN-KEY" BASIS

PREVIOUS PAGES: Formula 1 qualification was a chess game in the 1980s. Drivers would head out and try for a quick lap or two, then head back into the pits, where adjustments were made. While waiting, timing monitors would be placed in front of the drivers so they could keep track of where they, and the competition, stood. Benetton-Ford driver Thierry Boutson rests during such a lull in qualifying. Boutson would finish third in the '88 race.

ABOVE LEFT: Satoru Nakajima rests for a moment during practice for the 1987 race. The Japanese driver came to the Lotus team as part of the agreement for the Honda engines that helped propel teammate Ayrton Senna to the Detroit win that year, his second in a row. Nakajima was routinely a second or two slower than his Brazilian teammate.

ABOVE RIGHT: Arrows driver Marc Surer heads out of the pits following a qualifying session in the rain in 1983. Through the AP, I was assigned to cover Surer for a Swiss newspaper and followed him for the two days of practice and qualifying. Surer finished eighth in 1982 and 10th in 1983.

ABOVE: Conversations between drivers and their crew members were the focal point of much of my photography during practice and qualifying. Derek Warwick, seated in his Arrows-Megatron, was explaining his point to a crew member prior to qualifying for the 1987 race.

OPPOSITE: With his Alfa Romeo fitted with rain tires, Mauro Baldi waits for his turn to take to the track during qualifying for the 1983 race. Of note is that the pit space next to him for teammate Andrea de Cesaris is empty. Typically, the two-car teams would send just one of their drivers out at a time or try and stagger their times on the track to cut down on traffic.

LEFT: Patrick Tambay waits in his Ferrari in the rain during qualifying for the 1983 race. Tambay got the Ferrari ride after the death of Gilles Villeneuve in 1982 and eventually had success with the Prancing Horse. But 1983 was not his year in Detroit. He stalled his Ferrari on the grid, ending his race right there on the starting line.

- 51 -

OPPOSITE: Didier Pironi was the lone Ferrari entrant in the 1982 race after his teammate Gilles Villeneuve was killed just a month earlier. Patrick Tambay had been announced as Villeneuve's replacement, but he did not race in Detroit. Tragically, Pironi would be injured two months later at Hockenheim in Germany, ending his Formula 1 career. Five years after that, Pironi was killed in a boating accident.

ABOVE LEFT: It's hard to know which is more famous, the scarred face of three-time world champion Niki Lauda or the Parmalat Racing hat he wore. He is the man who came back from the dead and forever wears the scars from his fiery crash at the German Grand Prix in 1976. For me, he represented the very knife edge that was Formula 1 during the 1970s and '80s. Tragedy always seemed to be just around the corner.

ABOVE RIGHT: This photo was widely published. A large number of newspapers around the world ran it in stories about the first Detroit Grand Prix and some of the hiccups that occurred: the course not being ready, the numerous manhole covers on the course, and in general, the drivers not being satisfied with the layout. Ingenious caption writers went to work talking about how the three-time world champion was bored to be in Detroit. Maybe that was true, as Lauda never really had a good run in Motown. In his three appearances driving for McLaren, he failed to finish a race.

OPPOSITE: Nigel Mansell the gymnast. After going over the track wall to take care of a little business—a "pit stop" into the Detroit River—Mansell hops back over the track wall to head to the pits. Doing such a maneuver with a helmet on is not as easy at it looks. And they say race car drivers are not athletes.

LEFT: Nigel Mansell cools off following a practice run in his Lotus in 1984. As I was making this photograph, one of the Sports Car Club of America marshals asked Mansell if he wanted them to remove me from his pit box. Mansell replied, "Woman, are you daft? See all these patches on my uniform? They pay me to be sure these blokes take my picture. So go away." I have never liked a race car driver more than at that very moment.

OPPOSITE: Ferrari driver Rene Arnoux is escorted down pit lane by security guards after winning the pole for the 1983 race. His terrific smile says it all.

ABOVE LEFT: Nigel Mansell checks the monitor to see the qualifiers. Of all the photos I shot during the seven years of Formula 1 racing in Detroit, the two people I have the most photos of are Mansell and Ayrton Senna. Senna won the race three times, so it's easy to understand why he was in front of my lens so often. Despite never winning the Detroit race, Mansell was a daring qualifier who normally put his car up front on the grid.

ABOVE RIGHT: Rene Arnoux waits for service on his Ferrari prior to qualifying for the 1984 race. I have always liked this photo for Arnoux's posture and how he doesn't seem to have a care in the world as he waits for tires to be fitted to his race car.

CHAPTER 3

THE CHAMPIONS

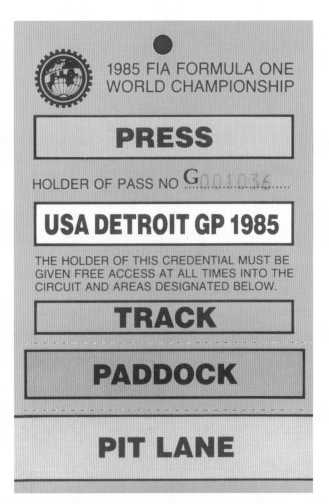

Could this innocent-looking youngster
be the same cutthroat driver that teammates—and opponents—loved to hate?
Yes, he's one and the same. Ayrton Senna
was master of the Detroit street course.

OPPOSITE: John Watson came into Detroit in 1982 knowing the Cosworth-powered McLarens he and teammate Niki Lauda were driving had a chance to do well on the tight, slow street circuit. But Watson qualified 17th on the grid with Lauda a few places farther up in 10th, and he truly thought he had no chance of winning. But come race day, Watson had one of the more spectacular drives ever in Formula 1 to win the inaugural Detroit Grand Prix.

ABOVE: John Watson's victory in Detroit in 1982 propelled him into the lead in the championship points race at that point in the season. At season's end he would find himself in second behind Keke Rosberg. Watson's drive from 17th starting position to the winner's circle was the most places anyone had made up; Jackie Stewart won the 1973 South African Grand Prix from 16th. Watson's drive in Detroit was one for the record books.

OPPOSITE: Michele Alboreto relaxes on the pit wall before practice for the 1987 race. The tape on his right hand protected it from blistering because of all the gear changes necessary on the tight street circuit. Alboreto was the 1983 winner driving a Cosworth-powered Tyrell, the last win for the venerable Cosworth DFV engine. In 1984, Alboreto moved to Ferrari, the first Italian in more than 10 years to drive for the Prancing Horse. He had one other podium finish in Detroit, taking third in 1985.

LEFT: In 1985, Ferrari driver Michele Alboreto came to Detroit, having won the week before in Canada. He followed that win with a good drive, finishing third behind Keke Rosberg and Stefan Johansson. He would go on to win again later in the year in Germany and eventually finish second in the world championship to Alain Prost. After the 1988 season, he was out of F1 and moved on to sports cars. He died in 2001 testing an Audi R8 sports car at the Lausitzring in Germany.

POSTCARDS FROM DETROIT

OPPOSITE: Keke Rosberg came to the 1986 Detroit Grand Prix as the defending champion, having won the previous year in a Williams-Honda. But for '86 Rosberg had jumped from Williams to McLaren-TAG Porsche, where he was teamed with Alain Prost. Rosberg failed to finish the race, as a gearbox failure sent him to the sidelines. He retired at the end of the season.

TOP RIGHT: Keke Rosberg, the 1985 winner, always seemed to be the coolest guy in pit lane, chatting up everybody from mechanics to celebrities. His long hair, gold jewelry, and attitude seemed almost stereotypical of a Formula 1 driver. The 1982 world champion had a lengthy discussion with actor-turned-driver Paul Newman before the first Detroit race.

BELOW RIGHT: During the several wet practices and qualification runs during the seven years of the Detroit Grand Prix, it was not uncommon for drivers to climb from their cars after a run and head right out to the pit wall to watch their competitors navigate the course. Keke Rosberg seems duly impressed by what he sees.

OPPOSITE AND ABOVE LEFT: The first Detroit Grand Prix practice session had been slated for Thursday, June 3, as Motown had landed a Formula 1 race without ever having hosted another race event. The extra day of practice was scheduled to give everyone more time on the track. But the circuit was not ready, and in fact, it was not ready until late in the afternoon of Friday, June 4. Because of what were viewed as serious safety issues with the track—namely, not enough run-off areas in corners—there was talk of a driver boycott. To pass time, reigning world champion Nelson Piquet spent time catching a Frisbee and kicking a makeshift soccer ball.

ABOVE RIGHT: Nelson Piquet and Jochen Mass have a discussion before practice for the 1982 race. Piquet, the reigning world champion, would fail to qualify for the race. His turbo-powered Brabham BT50-BMW suffered from mechanical problems, and he ended up posting the slowest time of all and thus did not make the race. Pole winner Alain Prost was upset. "The world champion should be guaranteed a position," he said.

ABOVE: Even though Nelson Piquet failed to qualify for the 1982 Detroit race, in 1984 there was no question he was in P1. Piquet came to Detroit after a dominating drive to victory in Canada, and the expectations for the Brabham-BMW were high. Piquet put the car on pole, and then his race car was wrecked in a multicar crash at the start (see page 80). Piquet moved to his spare car—the same one he used for qualifying—and led flag to flag to win the third Detroit Grand Prix.

OPPOSITE: Despite failing to qualify for the inaugural Detroit Grand Prix, Nelson Piquet had a relatively good record in Motown. In 1983, he finished fourth, he won the race in '84, and he finished sixth, fifteenth, second, and seventeenth in the following years.

PREVIOUS PAGES: With Aryton Senna's Lotus displaying first-place stickers for his first Formula 1 victory in Portugal earlier in the year and for his teammate Elio de Angelis's win at San Marino, Senna talks with Lotus car designer Gerard Ducarouge during qualifying for the 1985 race. Senna stuck the turbocharged Renault-powered Lotus on pole, 1.2 seconds faster than his nearest challenger.

ABOVE LEFT: Ayrton Senna da Silva made his debut in the 1984 Detroit Grand Prix aboard a Toleman-Hart, having moved to Formula 1 after winning the F3 title the previous year. The aggressive determination behind the wheel that he would become known for was evident in Detroit, as he crashed the Toleman in practice and in the race finished in 19th position. It would be his worst finish in Detroit.

ABOVE RIGHT: Ayrton Senna shows his frustration at trying to sort out the bumpy, twisting Detroit track. But not to worry, the Brazilian put his Lotus on pole for the 1985 race, although he would fail to finish, crashing in turn 3 on lap 26. It would be the last Detroit race he failed to finish.

ABOVE LEFT: Ayrton Senna was always easy to spot either on the track or in the pits. On the track the bright yellow helmet trimmed in green (the colors of the Brazilian flag) was a dead giveaway. In the pits, it was the blue Nacional hat he wore.

ABOVE RIGHT: Ayrton Senna looks at the monitor charting qualifying times as race engineer Steve Hallam, with clipboard, and Lotus team boss Peter Warr, wearing glasses in the background, look things over. Few fans seemed to notice the action, as the box seats in the background are sparsely filled.

OPPOSITE: Here are Ayrton Senna and Eddie Cheever prior to qualifying for the 1987 race. Senna would end up second on the grid to Nigel Mansell. Senna won the race, Mansell was fifth, and Cheever finished sixth.

ABOVE LEFT: Ayrton Senna gets ready for qualifications for the 1987 race. Team Lotus had switched sponsorship to the Camel cigarette brand, and the familiar black and gold John Player Special livery was gone. Senna and team manager Peter Warr credited the active suspension of the Lotus-Honda for the victory on the bumpy streets of Detroit.

ABOVE RIGHT: With his arm hanging out the side, Ayrton Senna looks like he's ready for an afternoon cruise, which, of course, is exactly what he did in the last year of the Detroit Grand Prix. Senna put the McLaren-Honda on pole and beat teammate Alain Prost to the checkered flag.

OPPOSITE: Ayrton Senna sits in the car as the McLaren crew goes to work before qualifying in 1988. In order to keep the weight of the car down, small amounts of fuel were added for the two- or three-lap qualifying bursts that were common at the time. There were numerous reports that the fuel Senna had in his car was different from that used in teammate Alain Prost's McLaren.

ABOVE: In just a few short years, Ayrton Senna had gone from a rookie to a respected member of the fraternity, with journalists seeking his comments at every step. He stopped along pit lane to talk with a television crew and immediately drew a crowd of other journalists.

CHAPTER 4

THE RACE

FIA
FORMULA 1
WORLD
CHAMPIONSHIP

RESTRICTED
AREA CONTROL

TRACK

U.S.A. G.P. 1988
PRESS

ROGER HART

PIT LANE

PADDOCK

PASS NO.
533288
FRI   SAT   SUN
①   ②   ③

I was asked to shoot several standard photos at each Detroit Grand Prix, and this was one of them. The assignment was to perch outside the track along the main straightaway that ran along the Detroit River, frame a car with the Renaissance Center rising in the background, and make the picture. Here, Ayrton Senna, in his first appearance in Detroit driving for the Toleman-Hart team, is shown during practice.

ABOVE AND OPPOSITE: For decades the start of a Formula 1 race has been the most exciting and the most dangerous in motorsports, as exemplified by the start of the 1984 race. And nowhere in American racing could photographers and spectators, many of whom are shown here running for cover, get this close to a racetrack. Nelson Piquet, on pole, was slow to start, and Nigel Mansell, coming up fast from behind, bumped Piquet into the wall, where he was hit hard by Marc Surer's Arrows. Piquet's front wheel was ripped off the car and bounced across the track, hitting the Toleman-Hart of Ayrton Senna and damaging his front suspension. The race was immediately red-flagged, and Piquet and Senna jumped into backup cars for the restart. Piquet went on to win the race. Amazingly no one—spectators, photographers, or drivers—was injured.

PREVIOUS PAGES AND RIGHT: Formula 1 races are often won at the start, and here a drag race between Ayrton Senna in a Lotus and Nigel Mansell in a Williams was won by Senna, who went on to win the 1986 event, the first of three in a row for the Brazilian. Mansell, who had a back-and-forth battle with Senna for the pole position the day before, went on to finish fifth. Mansell never won in Detroit.

In 1987, Nigel Mansell got a clean start away from the pack and led everyone into turn one. But Ayrton Senna, driving the Camel-sponsored Lotus, would eventually hunt Mansell down and pass him to win the second of his three consecutive Detroit races.

BELOW RIGHT: Nelson Piquet (car no. 7) in his Brabham-BMW closes in on the RAM-Hart of Phillipe Alliot along the main straight during practice for the 1985 race. Piquet, a three-time world champion, came into the race as defending champion but could manage only sixth place this year, one lap behind winner Keke Rosberg.

ABOVE: This is one of two photos I was responsible for taking on race day. Here, Ayrton Senna in his McLaren heads into the first turn with the crowded grandstands and the gleaming Renaissance Center in the background. With thousands of people packing downtown on a Sunday afternoon, Detroit rarely looked better.

ABOVE: Nelson Piquet aboard his Brabham-BMW backup car rounds the first corner after winning the 1984. A couple of the corner workers inside the track salute the Brazilian as he passes by.

OPPOSITE: One of the major concerns when the race course was laid out for the Detroit race was the possibility of a race car ending up in the Detroit River. This never happened, and in reality, it was never even close. But just in case, a Detroit Fire Department fire boat, replete with divers, was on hand and is seen here in the background as Nelson Piquet in a Williams-Honda races down the main straight. Also in the background is the Ambassador Bridge that links Detroit with Windsor, Ontario, Canada—adding another "international" touch to the event.

RIGHT AND OPPOSITE: In 1987, several cars ran titanium rub strips along the bottom of the chassis to protect the machines as they pounded over the rough streets of Detroit, with each impact causing a shower of sparks to flow from the back of the car. The sparks were worse when the cars were heavy with fuel. Here, Nigel Mansell's Williams-Honda makes sparks along the front straight during practice and then in the race in front of Ayrton Senna's Lotus-Honda.

BELOW RIGHT: Ayrton Senna aboard his McLaren-Honda rounds the corner in front of Cobo Hall during practice for the 1988 race. Due to a paperwork mistake, I was unable to get my credentials in time to be in the pits when F1 practice began, and I had just come out of Cobo Hall, where credential registration was located, when the first cars were on track. I stopped and made several frames—the only time in seven years I was out of my "normal" position.

ABOVE: Niki Lauda leads Keke Rosberg down the front stretch during the 1983 race. Most of the front stretch was a parking lot for the other 51 weeks of the year, but for the race weekend crews would paint over the parking lot stripes in preparation for the race.

OPPOSITE: Michele Alboreto in a Ferrari heads out of the chicane and down the front straightaway during a wet qualification run. Despite lap times several seconds slower than in dry conditions, it was truly amazing to see these cars running flat-out in the rain. It was something you would never see in American oval-track racing.

LEFT: In the first year of the race, Formula 1 cars didn't get onto the track until nearly 4 p.m. because of a variety of problems with runoff areas and tire barriers. Just a few minutes after that, Rene Arnoux stuffed his Renault into the turn two wall. This crash, and the efforts by the towing crew who were supervised by Arnoux, pointed out another problem—no cranes to remove wrecked cars.

BELOW LEFT: Safety marshals extinguish a fire that broke out on Ricardo Patrese's Brabham after a three-car crash during the inaugural Detroit Grand Prix. Through a cutout in the fence, photographers record the event. This crash, which also involved Roberto Guerrero and Elio de Angelis, forced the race to stop as the wreckage was cleared. The stop allowed eventual race-winner John Watson to make a tire change that is credited for his win.

TOP RIGHT: Ivan Capelli works to remove himself from his wrecked March-Judd along the inside pit wall during practice the day before the 1988 race. Several people along pit lane were injured by flying debris. Capelli broke a bone in his foot in the mishap and was unable to make the race.

BELOW RIGHT: Dangling from the hook of a wrecker, Ivan Capelli's March-Judd is hauled from the track, emphasizing the unforgiving nature of the concrete walls that lined the Detroit circuit.

BELOW: I attempted to make this photo each year—the race winner taking the checkered flag. Of my seven years of shooting this photo, this one from 1982 was the best. I'm sure John Watson would agree. Race winner Watson raises his fist as he crosses the line, and the checkered flag is nicely backlit, making it easily visible.

ACKNOWLEDGMENTS

Putting together this book has been a wonderful experience
for me, and there are many people who have made the process
a lot of fun. I would like to thank my wife, Lisa, who has been
my best editor for 25 years. Thanks to everyone at David Bull
Publishing; you exemplify the word "professional." To the
Associated Press and the staff at The Image Gallery in Adrian,
Michigan, thank you for your efforts.

Also, I owe a debt of gratitude to former AP photographers
Dale Atkins and Rob Kozloff, who gave a young, enthusiastic
photographer a chance to shoot big-time auto racing. What
you did for me professionally pales in comparison to something I value even more: our friendship.

ABOVE: Roger Hart, right, with AP photographer Dale Atkins in the Turn 1
tower prior to the 1986 Detroit Grand Prix.